It is
the kindest act
of love you will ever be
asked to perform!

love & light Ph. Wahhi

Wishing You...

DR. LAUREN NAPPEN
ah-h-h-justing to life

Headline Books, Inc.
Terra Alta, WV

Wishing You...

By Dr. Lauren Nappen

To order additional copies of this book or for book publishing information, or to contact the author:

Headline Books, Inc.
P. O. Box 52
Terra Alta, WV 26764
www.headlinebooks.com
www.ahhhjustingtolife.com

Tel: 800-570-5951
Email: mybook@headlinebooks.com

ISBN 978-0-938467-14-4

Library of Congress Control Number: 2011935001

PRINTED IN THE UNITED STATES OF AMERICA

To each of our paths and the willingness to walk them...

Love • Light

Here's to the return of your memory, to the sense of who you are, to the knowledge of what it is to

ah–h–h–just to life...

to open wide to that deep breath of inspiration that has sustained you through the ages, and awakens you to the generosity of the universe in all her forms, to finding out what makes you tick NOW (it might be different from yesterday,) to joy, to embracing all that Is, isn't, or might be...

And to the ONE true breath that encourages you to turn the page...

Wishing you Freedom

Magic

The use of a large, magic eraser to
wipe away the lines of constriction
that hold you hostage,
– lines drawn for
a thousand different reasons,
protecting a cavernous span of
memories and beliefs that remain
intact from habit, rather than necessity.

Wishing you Insight

Questions

Better questions for changing times, and answers that
remind you how to touch into your life.

Wishing you a New Perspective

Opportunity

The opportunity to re-think the shape of yourself by seeing every experience as a transformative one and welcoming how different you are and how good It all feels.

Wishing you Awareness

Grace

Grace and ease, as patterns that
no longer serve are relinquished to the
nothingness from which they came,
replaced with gratitude for realizing
they really were the best presents
ever bestowed upon you.

Wishing you Exhilaration

Adventure

Changes in your habitual life and
the potential to immerse yourself in
some 'off-center' adventure that
leaves you instantly awestruck.

Wishing you Humility

Cooperation

The essence of cooperation with
what IS and patience with what isn't.

Wishing you Stillness

Direction

An expansion of your Spiritual Sense of Direction,
by feeling and seeing and listening more
deeply through your heart to that thread
of truth that reveals your next steps,
all the while remembering that sometimes
the 'next step' is simply being still.

Wishing you Determination

Confidence

The capacity to follow your own lead
with confidence and courage
even though your chosen path makes
little sense to anyone else.

Wishing you Patience

Time

The remembrance that LIFE takes Time.

Wishing you Bravery

Willingness

The crazy courage to invade your own privacy
and watch the destruction of your most prized
and carefully crafted facades.

Wishing you the One Embrace

Surrender

*One complete moment of surrender so you'll know –
really, truly know – that the pristine beauty of your
Soul is the one embrace that lasts forever.*

Wishing you Discovery

Your Self

Hours and hours of hide and seek, only this time
You get to find yourself instead of someone else.

Wishing you Expansiveness

Hope

The chance to live your potential
instead of living your limitations.

Wishing you Enlightenment

Dawn

*Daily doses of enlightened darkness,
because the truth is that darkness precedes
the dawn every day, and this is your reminder
that the life you have led does not have to be
the only life you have.*

Wishing you Trust

Faith

The ah-h-h-ha moment that Relaxation
is merely Trust hiding in plain sight.

Wishing you Authenticity

Power

The courage to let truth telling be easy,
because it's not the truth that's scary;
rather it's the stuff we have
attached to telling the truth.

Wishing you an Abundance of Sweet Somethings

Behold

A box of cosmic Q-Tips to clean your ears so that when
God whispers 'sweet nothings' you'll recognize them as
'sweet somethings.'

Wishing you the Wilderness

Curiosity

The comfort to explore the wilderness of your dreams,
to embrace all that is unkempt, raw and creative...

Wishing you Intimacy

Sanctuary

*Intimacy with Compassion and the willingness
to be on the receiving end of her shelter.*

Tranquility

Permission to be at peace.

Wishing you Contentment

a Mirror

The shattering of your perceptual
tendencies that leave
you longing for something
outside yourself.

Wishing you Your Wings

Vision

The reminder that not every fall
will be cushioned, yet knowing
this somehow softens the edges,
strengthens the vision and inspires
you to jump regardless!

Wishing you Wisdom

Blessings

There is wisdom in changing your pace, experimenting with new rhythms, or exercising your inner flexibility with what stands before you. There is comfort in living more deliberately and full of care. To risk living fully into the unfolding adventure, lifting your feet from their resting place and letting Spirit take the lead is the ultimate point of surrender. Fluidity within the heart and spirit is an elegant way to honor the many textures within nature, within humanity. Now is the perfect time to receive the blessing of your own intrinsic beauty and individuality.

Wishing you Wonderment

Letting Go

At some point you will be offered the chance to let go...
...to let go of all that has kept you from raising yourself to
your highest level of attunement.

It's your truth or dare moment; just you and Spirit
participating in a dance that lives into eternity.

My wish for you is that you dare to live your truth in a
constant state of wonderment.

Wishing You

The return of your memory, to the sense of who you are, to
the knowledge of what it is to ah-h-h-just to life, to open wide
to that deep breath of inspiration that has sustained you
through the ages, and is the one true breath that encourages
you to turn the page, again and again and again.

**Dr. Lauren Nappen**, a natural born healer, chiropractor, spiritual intuitive, minister, visionary and witness has been encouraging people to rewrite their personal story for the past eighteen years by sharing the benefits and wisdom of alignment with Self and Spirit. She is the creator of various workshops and seminars, including Wellth of Soulutions, a monthly spiritual gathering that focuses on the joy of the soul.

Holding advanced certifications in a wide variety of healing disciplines, she currently shares her gentle ahhhjusting style and spiritual ministry at her healing sanctuary, *Ahhhjusting To Life*, in Bucks County, Pa. where she lives and works with her three black beauties, Riley, Emma and Oliver. Please visit her website at www.ahhhjustingtolife.com.